PICTURE

PUZZLER

BY KATHLEEN WESTRAY

TICKNOR & FIELDS BOOKS FOR YOUNG READERS

New York 1994

Published by
Ticknor & Fields Books for Young Readers
A Houghton Mifflin company, 215 Park Avenue South,
New York, New York 10003.

Manufactured in the United States of America

Book design by Kathleen Westray
The text of this book is set in 14 point New Baskerville
The illustrations are gouache, reproduced in full color

HOR   10   9   8   7   6   5   4   3   2   1

Library of Congress Cataloging-in-Publication Data
Westray, Kathleen.
Picture puzzler / by Kathleen Westray.   p. cm.
ISBN 0-395-70130-9
1. Optical illusions—Juvenile literature.
[1. Optical illusions.] I. Title.
QP495.W46 1994   152.14'8—dc20
94-4066   CIP   AC

For my sisters and brothers:
Rosemary, Maureen, Dickie, and David

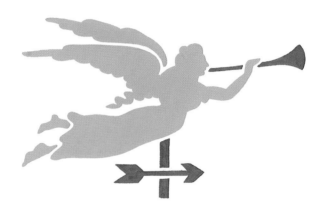

SEEING is believing—most of the time. But optical illusions play visual tricks. They can deceive or mislead us about what we see.

Some optical illusions, called afterimages, are caused by overstimulation of the eyes—the eyes get tired.

Stare at the intersections where the white lines cross. Gray dots will appear. These are afterimages. Stare at one dot and it will disappear. The dots around it will look darker.

Some afterimages are created by many lines that are spaced close together. Move the book from side to side and these closely spaced wavy lines seem to vibrate.

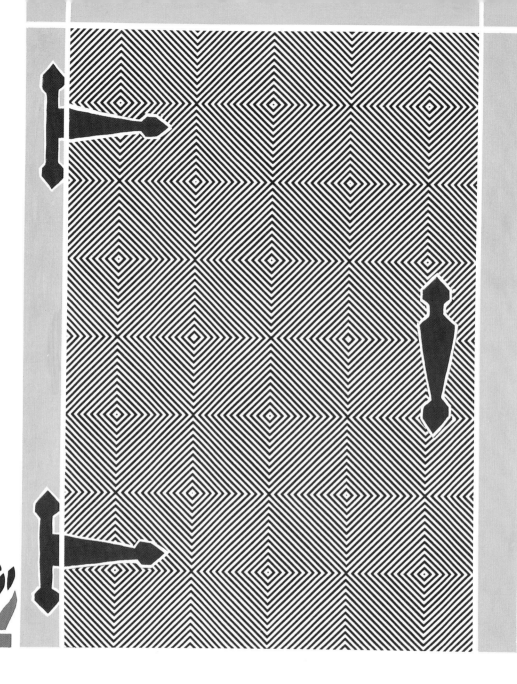

Look steadily at the door for a few seconds. Then blink and look again. The pattern keeps changing. Here, closely spaced straight lines create the illusion.

Stare at the wagon wheels. Moving shapes like the blades of a fan will appear. To make the wheels seem to turn, hold the book with both hands and keep moving it in a circular pattern.

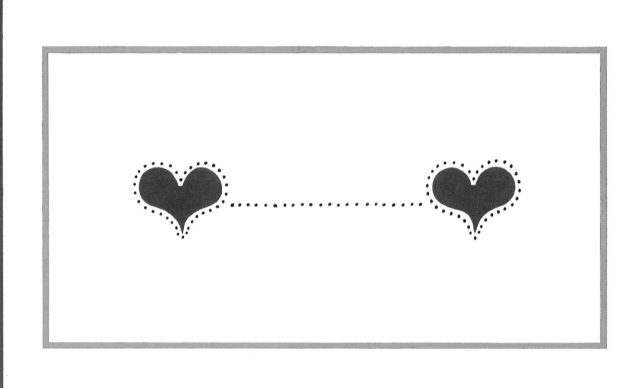

There is a small area in every eye called the blind spot, which cannot see anything. When both eyes are open, each fills in the other's blind spot.

To find the blind spot in your right eye, hold the book upright at arm's length. Close your left eye and focus on the heart on the left. Slowly move the book toward you until the heart on the right disappears.

Look at the space between the two unicorns. Slowly bring
the book toward you and watch the unicorns cross horns.
Since the eyes are a small distance apart, each has a slightly
different view. Up close, the two views begin to overlap.

Some optical illusions fool the brain as it tries to make sense of the images the eyes receive.

Using past visual experiences, the brain adds the missing parts to an incomplete picture. We "see" the complete tree even though there are no branches.

It is possible to find a white triangle in the middle of the picture. Look at the notches in the three black blocks. These are the corners of the triangle. The mind sees the rest of the triangle even without lines.

The brain tries to create patterns. These dots seem to be arranged in vertical columns because there is less vertical space between the dots than horizontal space.

The opposite is true for this pattern, so the dots seem to be arranged in horizontal rows.

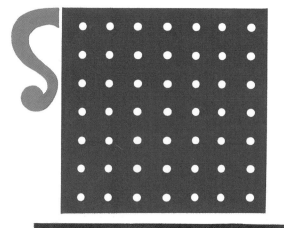

When all the dots are evenly spaced, they can be seen as either vertical columns or horizontal rows.

The many different circular patterns are dizzying. The brain cannot organize them into a single pattern.

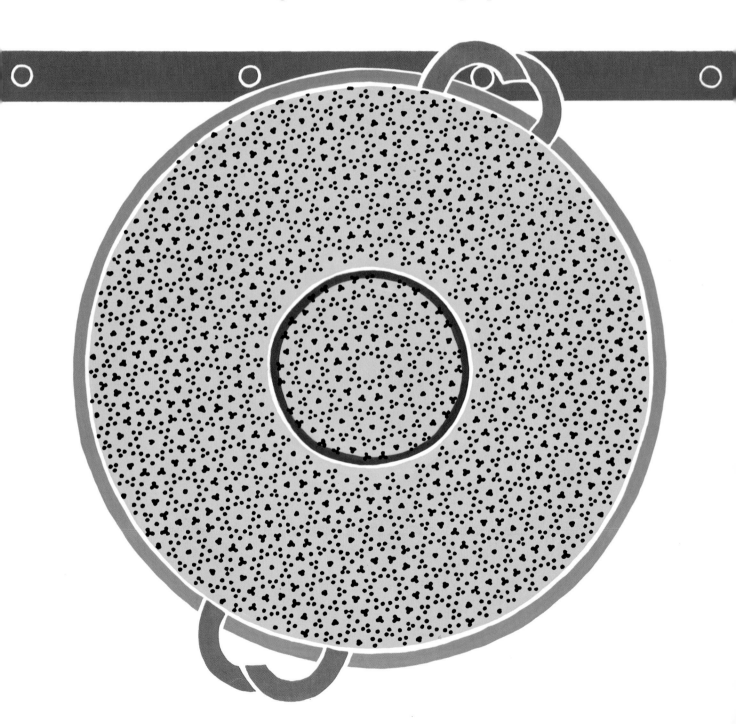

Visual illusions can create a sense of distance
and depth. As the slanting lines get closer
together, they seem to move into the distance.
As the birds get smaller, they, too, seem to move
into the distance. This is called perspective.

Which bird is larger? They are the same size. The perspective created by the slanting lines makes it look as if the top bird is farther away. Visual experience tells us that an object in the distance should look smaller than an object of equal size seen up close. The bird on top looks larger because of the way it has been placed in the drawing.

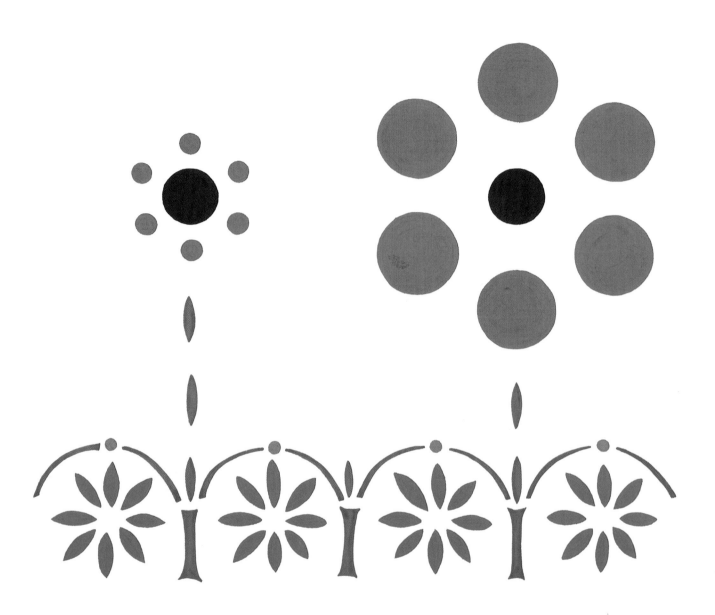

Comparisons can be tricky.

The two brown circles are the same size, but the one on the left looks bigger because we compare the brown circles with the other circles around them.

Which is longer: the hat itself, from top to bottom, or the hat's brim? They are the same length, but when we see a horizontal line and a vertical line together, the vertical line usually appears to be longer.

Color can be deceptive, too.
   The orange patterns on the sock are the same color. They look like different shades of orange because the colors next to them are different.

White is a bright color that seems to spread, making
the white flowers look bigger than the black ones.

Some optical illusions are created by distracting lines or shapes. All these vertical lines are straight. The diagonal lines make them appear to be tilting.

The two dark horizontal lines are straight. The white lines are distracting, creating the illusion that the dark lines are curving together.

Both of these pictures show either a vase or two faces,
depending on whether the eyes focus on the light or dark
shapes. When a picture's foreground and background

are equally strong it is possible to alternate what is seen. The shape focused on moves into the foreground, and the other drops into the background.

This single shape can be seen as two different images:
a duck facing left, or a rabbit facing right.

Some pictures are reversible. Is this the cover or
the inside of a book?

This is another reversible drawing. The lid can open toward the front or toward the back of the box.

Look at the red tops of the stack of boxes—the row of diamond shapes. Now look at the lowest row of red diamonds and imagine these are the bottoms of the boxes. Look slowly up the stack: all the boxes have reversed. It is impossible to see both ways at once.

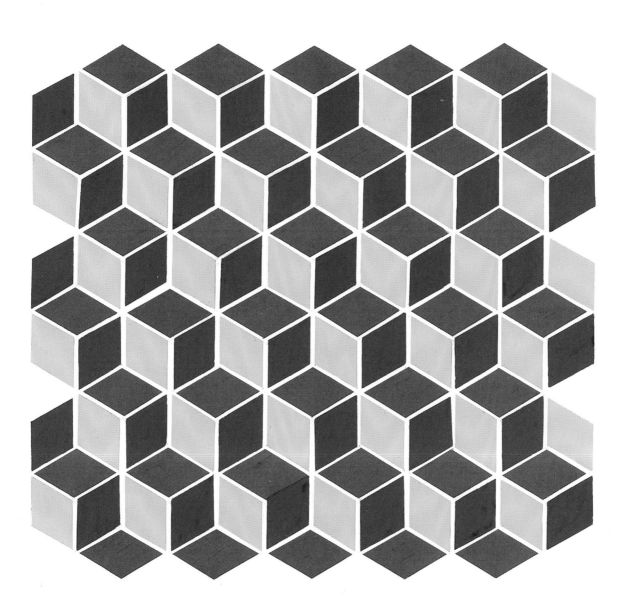

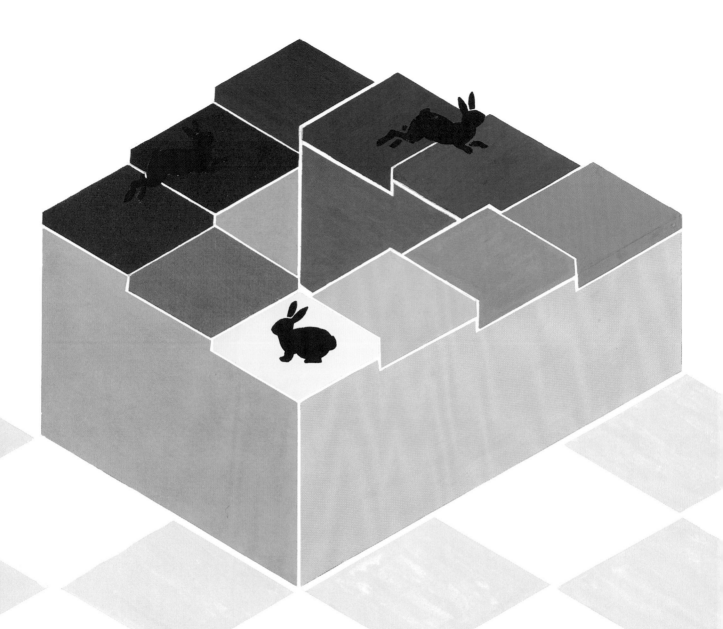

Trick drawings are pictures that look real but are impossible.
These never-ending stairs could not be built. Start on the
yellow step and move clockwise. The stairs seem to keep
going up, but they end back on the bottom yellow step.

This candleholder is also a trick drawing. The lines create the shape of three candles, but where is the middle one attached?

Objects can be hidden by their surroundings. This pair
of birds has nine fledglings. Where are they hiding?
  Optical illusions can fool the eyes and the brain. But
look carefully, and try to see behind the illusions.